The Five Financial Foundations

*A Guide to Building
a Better Future*

Jeff C. Johnson, CFP®

Infusionmedia
Lincoln, Nebraska
Since 1994

Infusionmedia
140 North 8th Street #214 The Apothecary
Lincoln, NE 68508-1353
www.infusionmediadesign.com

Printed in the United States

10 9 8 7 6 5 4 3 2 1
First Edition

ISBN: 978-0-9843101-9-7
Library of Congress Control Number: 2012955333

The Five Financial Foundations: A Guide to Building a Better Life is also available as an e-book at www.fivefinancialfoundations.com.

Jeff C. Johnson
Executive Wealth Management
6940 O Street, Suite 300
Lincoln, NE 68510

CONTENTS

PREFACE

If every American embraced the Five Financial Foundations, your world would probably be a better place to live and work. Sure, you might not be able to immediately buy everything you want if you follow the simple guidelines in this book, but your stress levels might be lower and your future security might be much higher.

Frankly, if everyone followed the Five Financial Foundations, the credit meltdown and recession that started in 2008 would probably not have occurred, at least not for the same reasons.

The Five Financial Foundations was developed over the last 30 years as a result of my life as a stockbroker, financial planner, and teacher. By observing real people who intuitively applied these basic principles, I was able to learn the simple secrets to working toward building a secure financial life.

Best of all, I learned that these people almost always benefited in non-financial ways—less work and worry as life progressed, happy marriages and family situations, and a calm that is the result of having a sense of what I call "Financial Confidence."

Many years ago I started crafting the short list of these traits and used it informally with people that came to me for counsel on ways to begin saving and investing. Then a few years ago I started teaching a personal finance class at the University of Nebraska-Lincoln, and I decided to build the entire course around the Five Financial Foundations.

The result has been a chorus of thank-yous from my former students who tell me they feel they are empowered by these simple rules and are motivated to start building a firm foundation for the future.

Please note, there is no "one size fits all" when it comes to financial planning. At some point many American savers and investors should seek the advice of a professional financial adviser and develop a custom, personalized plan of their own.

However, for someone just getting started or for someone with no plan at the present, these Five Financial Foundations are a great basis for further development.

I wrote this book for Americans everywhere that want a bigger and better future, both in their financial and nonfinancial lives.

CHAPTER 1

How I Discovered the Five Financial Foundations: The Story of the Surgeon and the Bookkeeper

---

For over 30 years I've observed and learned from my clients—some taught me what to do; from others I learned what not to do.

The Five Financial Foundations concept was developed entirely from my unscientific observation of people that I have advised or known professionally. The Bookkeeper and the Surgeon are fictitious and any resemblance to any one person is merely a coincidence, but each is based on the financial management traits of a number of real people I have known.

This is the story that I use as an example in my personal finance class at the University of Nebraska-Lincoln.

The Story of the Bookkeeper and the Surgeon

I met the Bookkeeper in the early 1980s when I made an in-person stop at his office and asked him to open an investment account with my firm, which he eventually did.

He had graduated from a two-year "school of commerce" and had started working for a local company. He and his wife had three young children, lived in a nice but decidedly middle-class home, and drove late-model used cars. His initial transaction with my firm was $2,000 placed in a very conservative investment.

Over the years he added to his portfolio and never withdrew or sold investments because he always had a substantial cash reserve "emergency" fund. When a relative left him a small inheritance, he added the entire sum to his account. He always pointed to the investing of this "windfall" as the event that really got his portfolio moving.

When he made purchases, he never borrowed the money, always paying cash that he had accumulated for the purchase. Big expenditures were always preplanned.

As his income grew and his family obligations were reduced, he was able to accelerate his spending and his saving. Since he and his wife wanted for little, they spent some and also increased their savings rate.

Almost 30 years later the Bookkeeper and his wife are living in the same comfortable home and have few financial concerns. Their children are all married and doing well on their own, saving money and building their own financial worlds.

At age 60 the Bookkeeper's net worth is at least $5 million, far more than he will need to live comfortably for life. He never earned a large salary, and his wife, a full-time homemaker, never worked outside the home but volunteered for important community projects. They give generously to charities (usually anonymously) and make practical financial gifts to their children and partially fund college savings accounts for grandchildren.

In my mind, they are very wealthy in every respect.

The Surgeon, whom I had known by reputation for many years, came to me shortly before his retirement and asked me to help him organize his income streams in anticipation of withdrawing from his practice. I was eager to work with a high-profile professional, well-known in our community.

He and his wife were the parents of three children, well educated at the best private universities, and they lived in a lovely custom home they had designed and built a few years before. They drove new luxury cars and enjoyed a high social image.

When the time came to review his finances, I discovered a problem. After earning millions in his professional career, he had accumulated only enough money to provide five or six years of retirement income at the level he had identified as a "livable" amount.

Additionally, there were significant credit card debts and a second mortgage on the home. The cash in his savings account was barely enough to make next month's payments. After earning millions in this professional career, his net worth was less than half of the Bookkeeper's net worth.

My recommendation involved a drastic reduction in spendable income for the rest of his life, as well as the sale of the custom home, "rightsizing" to a much smaller home, and the elimination of a number of expensive involvements and pastimes.

The Bookkeeper is the pattern for the Five Financial Foundations, the topic of this book. The Surgeon is an example of someone who could not find the discipline to use common-sense rules for the handling of his finances, expecting that his high income would last forever.

It's probably easy to imagine a bookkeeper who is thrifty and has intuitively developed a plan for saving and investing. In fact, people who have traits like the Bookkeeper in my story came from all walks of life and every level of income.

However, it's a common mistake to look at high-income people living a high lifestyle and incorrectly assume they are wealthy. Sadly, they not only have financial problems ahead but often end up suffering from nonfinancial issues.

Chapter 2 is an overview of the Five Financial Foundations that you can implement to work toward building a financially stable lifestyle.

A note to all the thrifty and financially astute physicians and surgeons I know and advise: I admire your ability to earn, save, and build wealth.

CHAPTER 2

Five Financial Foundations: The Overview

The Five Financial Foundations are simple, and that's what makes this book and this approach to building your financial future especially useful. Anyone who really wants a bigger and better financial future can do it by using these five financial guidelines and just getting started.

The Five Financial Foundations

1. Save some amount of money every time you get paid.

   An initial target savings rate is 10 percent of your earnings if you are able. If you are just getting started, a lesser percentage is OK. The most important thing to do is to begin, and to get used to, saving money.

2. Always have a cash reserve for emergencies and future larger consumer goods purchases (such as a car, furnishings, etc.) so you won't have to borrow money and pay interest.

   This amount can vary depending on a person's situation, but an initial target is one to two months' living expenses as a minimum; later in life, a full year's living expenses should be held in reserve.

3. Take full advantage of tax-favored investment accounts, such as your employer's retirement savings plan, an IRA, or a Roth IRA.

   These long-term savings vehicles are where most regular people can build their largest pools of wealth.

4. If you decide to own a home, the purchase price should be no more than two to two-and-a-half times your household income.

    Save and accumulate at least 20 percent of the purchase price for a down payment and finance the balance with a long-term fixed-rate mortgage.

5. No consumer (or "bad") debt.

    Bad debt is high-interest, nontax-deductible, and is used to pay for things of no value or declining value, such as clothing, entertainment, and vacations.

That's it. Pretty simple, really ... but not easy to implement. It takes discipline, and it will require denying yourself some material items that you think you want. You may have convinced yourself that you need these items, but in reality they are a temporary want and are something you will have to forgo.

The basis for all self-accumulation of money starts with this formula:

$$Spending < Earnings$$

Spend less than you earn. Or, find a way to earn more than you spend.

This information is nothing new; it's old and timeless wisdom. Paraphrasing Benjamin Franklin:

"There are two ways of being happy ... diminish our wants or augment our means... and if you are wise you will do both at the same time..."

That leads us to the next chapter: learning to save something every time you get paid, the first of the Five Financial Foundations.

CHAPTER 3

Banking Every Time You Get Paid:
Exercising Your Saving Muscles

Save some amount of money every time you get paid.

"Spend less than you earn" seems simple enough, but it is difficult to do in today's world for many reasons.

Here's how to get started if you haven't developed a saving habit.

Learning to save money is not unlike getting into physical condition. Imagine you want to get physically fit, and the first day you set out to run five miles. How do you think you would fare? Do you think it would be likely that you would not be able to complete your anticipated five-mile run? The next day would you be sore or even injured and unable to run again for days or maybe weeks?

The better way might be to start with a jog around the block every day for a week, then increase to two laps around the block, building up to a greater distance and a bigger workout, leading to better physical conditioning.

The same is true for the person who wants to attempt to get into better financial condition. Rather than take a thick slice out of your next paycheck, you might be better off by saving a smaller, more manageable amount and to start increasing your savings from there to a more meaningful savings goal.

How much is enough to start saving? That depends on your situation.

If you're a student in my college personal finance class, you might start by saving from your part-time job. Are you a server or a bartender? Maybe you can start with my recommended initial savings rate right away (10 percent if possible) or maybe all you can afford is $1 or $2 every day or night you work.

Just start with an amount you can stick with at regular intervals. You can always increase it from there as you build your "saving muscles." The greatest problem for many people who do not save seems to be just getting started.

Later, as your earnings rise, an increase in savings to 20 percent or 30 percent is recommended. Some prolific savers I know save over 50 percent of their earnings.

To start, saving 10 percent is all about adjusting your standard of living to 90 percent of what it could be and banking the remaining 10 percent.

Where should the money saved be directed?

If you do not have cash reserve, a savings or money market account should be the first place you consider funding (the topic of the next chapter).

After building some emergency monies, you can begin investing for the long term by starting or increasing your payroll deduction at work, funding the retirement plan offered by your employer. Frequently the plan available at work offers matching contributions that could be "free money" you won't want to miss out on. IRAs and Roth IRAs also provide long-term tax-advantaged accumulation opportunities.

If you are working to reduce some lingering debts, you might want to consider saving a smaller amount while sending a larger chunk to pay off your credit card bills or other debts.

Many serious-for-the-first-time wealth builders have no cash reserve, no retirement savings, and debts that need to be paid off. It's been my experience that many "FFF First-timers" can benefit from addressing all three at once, in smaller, reasonable amounts.

As an example: The First-timer might be best off by sending 3–4 percent of earnings to pay down credit card debt principal (in addition to the minimum payment), 3 percent to a cash reserve savings account until it reaches a target balance, and 3 percent to the company plan, capturing an additional 3 percent from employer-matching payments.

Some people are intuitively able to find a way to save and build wealth. For many of us, it is more difficult to find that discipline. Regular saving can be assured by automating the savings, so that money is automatically transferred from your paycheck to a reserve account or an investment.

In the next chapter we will examine how, where, and why building a cash reserve is so important.

Initial Assessment

How are you doing on FFF #1? What is your present savings rate?

A. Your present annual earnings $ _____
B. Savings to all accounts over the past 12 months $ _____

Divide annual earnings (A) by annual savings (B)
to determine present savings rate   _____ %

Evaluate your saving behavior by checking one of the following:

❒ I am saving 10% or more from my earnings.
❒ I am saving but not consistently.
❒ I am not saving.

FFF #1 Goal: save a portion of all earnings, saving 10% of earnings as a beginning goal.

CHAPTER 4

Wood in the Shed: Why You Must Have a Cash Reserve

Always have a cash reserve for emergencies and future larger consumer goods purchases (such as a car, furnishings, etc.), so you won't need to borrow money and pay interest.

Everyone can benefit from building a cash reserve for future unplanned "emergency" expenses, as well as for planned spending on larger purchases, such as a car, a down payment on a home, or a family vacation.

Yet many, if not most, Americans do not have any meaningful amounts of cash available. This forces them to take financial actions that are not in their best interests, which usually means taking out high-interest loans that linger for years, often costing more in interest than the original loan principal.

It could mean relying on parents or other family members to "help out," which sometimes strains family relationships. Lack of cash might require the forced sale of potentially valuable assets or investments prematurely; it might lead to missed opportunities.

Without cash reserve there is a lack of "Financial Confidence."

How much cash is enough?

Deciding how much cash reserve should be on hand is often more of an art than a science, but here are my formulas:

If you're just starting out or have never saved money, build up to one to two months' living expenses as quickly as you can. As you save more in retirement plans and pay off debts, increase your cash reserves.

Unable to determine what your monthly expenses are? I suggest that my college students, who don't always have a good handle on their living costs, to target 10 percent of their expected salary for the next year as an amount to get started.

As your financial situation improves, bump up your reserve to six months' living expenses and add amounts for purchases that you plan to make in the next years.

Targeting Your Cash Reserve: How Much Is Enough?

Example: Your known monthly expenses are $3,000, and you know you will soon need $10,000 to trade up to a better-running car.

Basic Six Month Reserve (6 × $3,000)	$18,000
Future Car Purchase	$10,000
Target Cash Reserve	$28,000

Later in life or in retirement, the amount of cash reserve should be twelve months' known living expenses plus any potential large purchases or expenditures.

It requires discipline and a desire to get ahead to build up a cash reserve. But the choice to live in a thrifty or even frugal manner is a decision to trade a "spendy" live-for-today lifestyle for a secure life for you and the people most important to you.

To be clear, what this means is forgoing the momentary pleasure of purchasing material goods (unnecessary consumer items of quickly evaporating value) and in return eventually living a comfortable life with "financial confidence."

The accomplished saver learns to build cash and to preplan for all large expenditures, in addition to having an emergency fund.

This cash reserve should be held in a secure account with instant liquidity and no volatility in price, such as a bank savings account or money market account. While some interest or return is desirable, any sacrifice of certainty for higher interest should be strictly avoided.

Your cash will probably not generate earnings anywhere near the return of your long-term growth investment accounts over time (the topic of the next chapter). But the reserve fund will make you money in the form of interest not paid on high-cost emergency loans.

You will also be able to afford to leave long-term investments untouched during difficult economic times, which could reward you with far greater returns than the modest interest paid on liquid cash and savings accounts.

For most of us that can't invent new software, can't act or play professional basketball, and are unable to perform like Lady Gaga, delaying spending and reducing lifestyle is a must, and the sooner in life you get started, the better off you'll be, as you will learn in the next chapter.

Initial Assessment

How are you doing on FFF #2? How many months of expenses do you have in cash reserve?

A. Amount of your liquid cash reserves $ _____
B. Your approximate monthly living expenses $ _____

Divide cash reserve (A) by living expenses (B)
to determine the number of months of expenses
you hold in reserve for an emergency   _____ mths.

Evaluate your cash liquidity by checking one of the following:

❐ I have a cash reserve that would be available in an emergency.
❐ I have some cash saved, but it is not adequate.
❐ I do not have a reserve fund for an emergency.

FFF #2 Goal: three to six months of living expenses as a minimum emergency fund.

CHAPTER 5

The Wealth-Building Workhorse: Your Biggest Pool of Money

Take advantage of tax-favored retirement plans, such as your employer's retirement savings plan, an IRA, or a Roth IRA.

This is a chapter that will touch on a number of concepts: long-term savings, stock market investment returns, tax deferral, retirement accounts, and compounding of money. I've added sidebars and extra resources for you to use to better understand and study these tools and concepts.

In the previous chapter we identified the need for a secure and immediately available cash reserve. The advantage is that you can quickly access your money in an emergency or for preplanned spending. The disadvantage is that the return on safe, liquid savings reserve accounts is normally well below the potential gains of long-held investments.

Tax-favored retirement accounts are the place where most of us regular Americans build our biggest pool of money. The reason is that we can invest this money for long periods of time and compound the growth for years and years. And of great importance is the ability to delay payments for income taxes on the money and the gains during this accumulation period.

Many of my college students (and many readers of this book) can reasonably expect to amass well over $1 million in their retirement accounts.

If you work for a company that provides a retirement savings plan, you can set up an automatic deduction from your earnings that goes directly into a retirement investment account. It's likely that this contribution can be deducted before income taxes, making it easier to save a larger amount of money.

Let me explain this with an example:

You make $40,000 per year and you decide to save 10 percent of your salary in your company retirement plan, deducted directly from your check before you get paid. In this instance, $4,000 would be transferred to the plan during the year, and at the end of the year you would report and pay tax on income of $36,000. The $4,000 was saved before it was taxed, and it will not be taxed until you withdraw it in retirement, allowing you to earn a return on the entire $4,000, potentially for many years.

Additionally, all the growth of the account and all the additional contributions to the account would benefit from delayed taxation. This money is free to grow, untaxed, until withdrawn for retirement income in monthly amounts, with the balance of the account continuing to grow tax-deferred during your retirement years.

Many company plans offer "matched" contributions, where the employer makes an additional contribution to the employee's account up to a specified limit, often 3 percent of the employee's earned income.

Using our example above, you earn $40,000 and contribute $4,000 to your plan account. If your employer matches 3 percent of earnings, you would get an additional contribution of $1,200 to your account (so long as you contribute at least the same amount).

Many Americans do not sign up to contribute to their company-sponsored retirement plans and miss out on this "free" matched contribution.

Retirement plans offer great tax advantages, as you can see, but in return there is a requirement that this money cannot be withdrawn or used until retirement, which is usually defined as no sooner than age 59 ½. Money that is withdrawn early is subject to full income taxation plus a 10 percent tax penalty.

Depending on your age when you begin retirement saving and the amount of time before you will retire from a working career, you could elect to invest in higher-growth investments that are offered by your plan. Growth investments in stocks are not guaranteed and will fluctuate in value. Sometimes the declines can be severe.

Before investing in stocks, you should study the history of stock market returns and understand that stock investments work best if made over periods of 20 years or longer. Consistently adding to your investment account, with monthly contributions, could also enhance your returns because during periods of inevitable downturns in prices, you are buying more shares at a lower price. This is much easier to accomplish with automatic payroll savings than having to make the decision to invest each month, when stocks are in a period of decline.

"What to Expect: The Historical Returns of the Stock Market" (an excerpt from a chapter from my book *The Extreme Retirement Planning Workbook: Navigating the Next 30 Years*)

There's a lot of information about stock market investing today. In fact, there is too much information, most of it bad, and most of it too confusing for investors to sift through and arrive at an appropriate decision.

Cable television channels, magazines, the Internet, and newspapers are packed with reports on a daily, even minute-to-minute, basis. There is more information and more choices; it's like drinking out of a fireman's hose!

What I'm not going to do in this chapter is to give you specific investment market returns. I'm also not giving you a prediction on the markets over the near term. But I am going to give you an easy research project that will help you to understand the need to be long term in your thinking.

Your research project

(1) Find an investment that has been continuously in business for at least 40 years. Use the Internet or your financial adviser to develop a list of candidates to study.

(2) During the life of the investment, determine how many years the investment gained and how many years the investment lost money.
   (a) Years with a gain
   (b) Years with a loss
(3) Next, using investment company hypothetical illustrations, look at all the rolling five-year historical returns during the life of the investment.
   (a) Five-year periods that gained
   (b) Five-year periods that lost
(4) Now do the same with rolling eight-year periods.
   (a) Eight-year periods that gained
   (b) Eight-year periods that lost
(5) Look at 20-year rolling historical returns.
   (a) 20-year periods that gained
   (b) 20-year periods that lost

What you are likely to learn from this exercise are the following:

(1) One-year returns are all over the map. Some very high returns are common; big losses are also common.
(2) The rolling five-year periods have a mostly positive result, but a few five-year periods (like the period that ended in 2008) would have lost money for stock investors.
(3) Eight-year periods are almost all positive, and the average annual returns of the periods are a little more predictable than the five-year historical.
(4) The 20-year periods were also almost all profitable, and the average annual return, even for the worst 20-year period, was decent.

> The point of this chapter is to help you understand the need to have a long-term perspective on your stock investments and to understand the range of outcomes that you could have earned on your portfolio over 20-year periods in the past.
>
> *Past performance is no guarantee of future results. All investing involves risk, including the potential to lose principal. Please discuss your specific situation with a qualified financial adviser prior to investing.*

Wealth-building investors always take advantage of tax-advantaged accounts like the company retirement savings plan as well as traditional and Roth IRAs. Find a way to get started now and work toward maximizing your savings up to the allowable contribution limits.

One reason that many Americans cannot save adequate amounts is because they own a house that is too expensive and they must make payments (and related home expenses) that are so large they cannot fully fund their wealth-building accounts.

The next chapter is about owning the rightsized home, a Happy House.

Roth IRA versus Traditional IRA

An Individual Retirement Account (IRA) is a tax-advantaged account that was designed to help Americans to save money for retirement. Over the years the rules and limits have changed, so here are the basics as of this writing (2012), but they are sure to change over time.

A traditional IRA features a deductible contribution (subject to income limitations). So, if you earn $40,000 per year and make a $1,000 contribution to your IRA, you would pay tax on $39,000 due to the deduction. More importantly, the investment will grow without any taxes due on the growth or the interest earned until the money is withdrawn at retirement, at which time it is taxable. This allows the saver to earn additional returns on the untaxed earnings, potentially for many years.

IRA contributions are limited to $5,000 per year ($6,000 if you are 50 years of age or older). You can only contribute to an IRA if you have earned income.

A Roth IRA has the same $5,000/$6,000 contribution limits, but the contribution is not deductible. However, the trade-off is this: the contributions and ALL EARNINGS in the account are withdrawn tax-free during retirement years. Wow!

Generally the traditional IRA is more advantageous for savers with higher taxable income who favor more conservative, lower-returning investments.

Roth IRAs are especially attractive for young savers early in their careers, who have lower tax situations where the deduction is less advantageous and who can consider high-growth potential investments.

There's no free lunch. Both the IRA and Roth IRA require that these investments be held until the IRA holder's age of 59 ½ or a tax penalty will apply to early withdrawals.

Banks, insurance companies, and many other financial institutions and investment firms offer IRA accounts, and many investment vehicles are available. The account grows or earns based on the investments selected within the IRA.

Earned income limitations apply to both the traditional and Roth IRA.

This is not a complete discussion of the topic. Speak with a qualified financial or tax adviser for specific details and learn how an IRA or Roth IRA could work best for you.

Initial Assessment

How are you doing on FFF #3? Are you making the most of tax-advantaged savings opportunities?

1. Are you eligible for a 401(k), 403(b), or other employer-sponsored retirement savings plan? ❏ Yes ❏ No

    A. If you are, how much have you accumulated in these accounts? $ _____
    B. How much will you add to these accounts in the next year? $ _____

2. Are you eligible to contribute to a Roth IRA or traditional IRA? ❏ Yes ❏ No

    A. If you are, how much have you accumulated in these accounts? $ _____
    B. How much will you add to an IRA this year? $ _____

3. Are you eligible to contribute to another tax-favored investment or savings account? ❏ Yes ❏ No

    A. What is the total amount you have accumulated in these tax-advantaged accounts so far? $ _____
    B. How much can you add to these accounts this year? $ _____

Evaluate your long-term savings vehicles by checking all that apply below:

❏   I am contributing to a 401(k) or similar employer-provided plan.

- ❒ I am investing through a company stock purchase plan.
- ❒ I am investing in a Roth or traditional IRA.
- ❒ I am accumulating cash value in a permanent life insurance policy.
- ❒ I am not participating in any long-term savings plans.

FFF #3 Goal: maximize your contributions to tax-favored investment alternatives.

CHAPTER 6

Happy House: Rightsizing Your Castle

If you decide to own a home, the purchase price should be no more than two to two-and-a-half times your household income.

There are some very good reasons why you should own a home. There are some very good reasons why you should *not* own a home, too. Ask yourself these questions:

Do you intend to stay in the community for a number of years? Are you comfortable staying in a house you are considering for purchase for a long period of time? Would you be better off with an apartment where you can simply move on if you uncover better economic or social opportunities? Would you be better off living in a rental property and saving some extra money for cash reserve and a future home purchase?

As an owner of your own home the advantages include the following: it's yours and you can do as you please, within reason; you lock in the cost of your housing if expenses rise due to price inflation, which has been common in America. At this writing mortgage interest rates are at very low levels and home prices might be attractive after several years of recession and an uncertain economy.

Still, your home may have many extra expenses, including real estate taxes, insurance costs, homeowner association fees, and maintenance and repair expenses that, in total, can exceed 10 percent of the value of the home each year. Often-mentioned advantages of homeownership are tax deductions and "equity buildup," neither of which is a strong reason to purchase a home.

Buying the right home is an extremely important decision. Be sure you get good advice and professional assistance if you are not knowledgeable about real property and especially if you are a first-time homebuyer.

It can be very easy to be swayed to purchase a house that is too expensive. Even if you can afford the mortgage, it could hamper your ability to build your cash reserve and your investment accounts because your money also has to meet tax and repair expenses, not to mention the purchase of home furnishings and decorating.

Based on economics in 2012, owning a "rightsized" home that is two to two-and-a-half times your annual household income is normally a better strategy. Here's an example:

You and your spouse earn $100,000. Based on the FFF formula, you can look for a home that is in the range of a $200,000 to $250,000 purchase price. To put yourselves on even firmer ground you should save at least 20 percent of the purchase price for a down payment, financing the balance on a long-term fixed-rate mortgage. A fixed-rate mortgage features principal and interest payments that will not change, even if interest rates rise.

Saving and accumulating 20 percent of the purchase price, in this example $40,000 to $50,000 dollars, could take years and would likely involving renting a home or apartment during the accumulation period.

Buying the largest home you can afford often leads to lack of savings and the steady accumulation of expensive consumer loans and credit card debts, the topic of our next chapter.

Mortgage Danger Zone: Variable-Interest, No-Interest, and Low-Down-Payment Mortgage Loans

Mortgage companies and lenders offer a number of innovative loans that make owning a home "more affordable," which means it allows home buyers to own a bigger, more expensive home (which is not always a good thing). Further, these loans have adjustable interest rates and payments, and many are available with little or no down payment required.

These flexible loans can make home ownership easier in the short term, but it can lead to serious trouble if rates rise or the borrower's financial situation changes.

Based on the low conventional mortgage rates at this time (late 2012), it makes good sense to follow the lead of the people who were the pattern for the Five Financial Foundations: seek long-term fixed-rate financing, with payments of principal and interest that will not change and will eventually fully pay off the loan. By making a 20 percent or greater down payment, the home buyer starts with significant equity in their home.

Initial Assessment

How are you doing on FFF #4? What percentage of your annual earnings is the value of your home?

A. If you own a home, what is the approximate value? $ _____

B. What is your total household income? $ _____

Divide your home value (A) by your household income (B) to determine your home-value-to-income ratio _____ %

Evaluate your home value and mortage by checking one of the following:

❏ I own my home free and clear, no mortgage.
❏ I own a home and have a mortgage that is less than 80% of home value.
❏ I own a home, but the mortgage is greater than 80% of the value of the home.
❏ I am renting and saving the difference between my rent and what a mortgage payment might be.
❏ I am renting but not saving.

FFF #4 Goal: if buying a home, the value of the property should not exceed two to two-and-a-half times your annual earnings. Your mortgage should not exceed 80% of the purchase price, and the interest rate should normally be fixed for the life of the mortgage loan.

CHAPTER 7

No Bad Debt: Avoiding an American Illness

Bad debt is high-interest, nondeductible, and used to pay for things of no value or declining value, such as clothing, furniture, entertainment, and vacations.

Americans have been lured into living consumer-oriented lifestyles, as if buying and owning the right stuff will make you happy.

Possessions rarely make anyone permanently happy, and as with other addictions, an addiction to possessions leads to bigger and bigger spending. Spending leads to debt; sometimes it leads to unmanageable debts.

Bad debt is produced by purchasing goods and services using a credit card, store card, or some other kind of borrowing tool. These purchases are items that do not have any value or will decline in value over time. The rate of interest charged on bad debt is often in excess of 18 percent per year. And, to make it worse, the interest expense is normally not deductible for income-tax reduction purposes.

Good debt, on the other hand, is used to make purchases that could increase in value or create more income or profit than the cost of the interest charged on the good debt. Because the purchase can add economic benefit over the long term, the interest charged is much lower and usually deductible against your income at tax time.

Typical good debt is used to purchase a home, a business, or an education that will benefit a student over a lifetime.

Well, that's it. You now know how to begin saving and building for your financial future. Now it is time to get started, the topic of our next chapter.

How Long Does It Take to Pay off a Credit Card Balance When Making the Minimum Monthly Payment?

Making on-time payments on your credit card is good for your credit rating. Making on-time *minimum* payments is horrible for your finances!

Why? Assuming 18 percent interest that is commonly charged on a credit card, the borrower making minimum payments would have to keep paying for up to 30 years to pay off the balance—imagine the amount of interest that would be paid!

Many Americans fall deeply into this trap, making minimum payments and continuing to charge to their credit cards, only to eventually realize they are so far in debt that they have crippled themselves financially.

If you have a credit card, you must realize that the first month you cannot pay off your balance in full, you are walking along the crumbling rim of a financial canyon, and you might fall in.

If you have built up some large balances on your credit cards, develop a plan to pay off the debt now. It could take you as long to pay off this debt as it took you to accumulate the debt. Seek the advice of a CERTIFIED FINANCIAL PLANNER ™ or a credit counselor if you need assistance figuring out how to restore your financial health.

Initial Assessment

How are you doing on FFF #5? Do you have "bad debt"?

A. Credit card balances (amount not paid off
    every month) $ _____

B. Department store card balance $ _____

C. Consumer loan(s) used to buy assets that
    decline in value $ _____

D. Automobile purchase loans $ _____

E. Other amounts you owe that have no
    business purpose $ _____

Total "bad debt" to be reduced and eliminated $ _____

Evaluate your debt status by checking one of the following:

❑   I have no consumer debt.

❑   I have some loan balances, but I am in the process of paying
off my debt.

❑   I have substantial credit card and consumer debt, and I need
a plan to pay off my debt.

FFF #5 Goal: no consumer debt.

CHAPTER 8

Getting Started Right Now

What if I have no savings, no cash, lingering credit card balances,
no home equity, and bills to pay?

Do something, right now, and take action immediately.

Sign up for your 401(k) or other savings plan at work. Can't afford it? Start with 1 or 2 percent of your earnings automatically taken from your payroll, and then increase it 1 or 2 percent every six months. Doing something, even if it is modest, is much better than doing nothing. If possible, sign up for the full amount of the employer match, often 3 percent. This way when you save 3 percent, you are really gaining 6 percent, doubling your money before receiving any investment returns.

> **A Tale of Two Savings Accounts**
>
> *An amazing lesson for college students and anyone under age 30*
>
> The money saved before age 30 could be more valuable than the money saved after age 30. If you are a 20-something (or know one), do not waste the opportunity to put money to work before you are age 30!

Consider this hypothetical example:

Joe starts saving $5,000 per year at age 20, using his savings to make annual investments of the same amount each year until age 29. This results in a total savings (before interest) of $50,000 in his "pre-age 30" account. This money is left to compound at 8 percent per year until he is age 70.

In a new account, Joe starts saving $5,000 per year at age 30 and does so for 40 years ($200,000 total invested), earning the same 8 percent per year until he is age 70.

Which of the two accounts is the most valuable at age 70?

Saving Account #1

Age	Amount Saved
20	$5,000
21	$5,000
22	$5,000
23	$5,000
24	$5,000
25	$5,000
26	$5,000
27	$5,000
28	$5,000
29	$5,000
Total Invested	$50,000
Account Value at Age 30	$72,432
Account Value at Age 70	$1,573,568

```
┌─────────────────────────────────────────────────────────────┐
│                                                             │
│   Savings Account #2                                        │
│   ─────────────────────────────────────────────────────    │
│                                                             │
│                    Age      Amount Saved                    │
│                   30-69     $5,000 per year for 40 years    │
│                                                             │
│            Total Invested   $200,000                        │
│       Account Value at Age 70   $1,295,282                  │
│                                                             │
└─────────────────────────────────────────────────────────────┘
```

No cash reserve? Open a savings or money market account and put a few bucks in the account every time you get paid. Increase this amount every six months.

Do you have debts to pay to credit card companies or other lenders? Start by making additional principal payments when you make your minimum payment and stop charging on the card until it is paid off. Do not close these accounts! Put the cards in an envelope, seal the envelope, and put it in a safe place until your debts are paid off. It will probably take you as long to pay off these debts as it did to accumulate them. Increase the principal payments every month if possible.

If you have high-interest, nondeductible "bad" debts, do not pay extra principal on your mortgage. You can start a prepayment program on your mortgage later when your expensive consumer debts and credit cards are paid off.

Find the "leaks" in your budget: start by looking at how much you spend on food and entertainment away from home. Next, examine your purchases of nonessential items. If you can identify spending that you can cut back in the amount of 5 or 10 percent of your total monthly pay, you are on your way to financial fitness.

Remember that building your "saving muscles" is much like getting physically fit.

Have an expensive car with debt or on lease? Explore ways to "trade down" to a less expensive, reliable used car.

Here's a getting started checklist:

- ❏ Open a savings account or deposit cash to an existing account.
- ❏ Resolve to always have $ _____ in cash for an emergency.
- ❏ Decide how much you will need for your next large purchase (car) and start saving so you can pay cash.
- ❏ Sign up for your 401(k) or other savings plan at work; bump up your savings rate if you are already participating.
- ❏ Assess your housing costs. Are they less than 20–25 percent of your income? Housing costs can include rent or mortgage, utilities, repairs, and association dues.
- ❏ Make a principal payment to a credit card and plan to pay it off before using it again.

How a College Student Can Have an Extra Million Dollars for Retirement

First, can you accept my logic that over 40-year periods of time, it could be possible to earn 10 percent per year on average, at least from a historical perspective? If you can imagine that this is possible, read on. If you cannot accept this possibility, undertake and complete the stock market research project in chapter 5.

Next, you need to understand that money that is invested for 40 years and left to compound at 10 percent grows 45 times. One hundred dollars invested today and earning 10 percent would be worth $4,500 in 40 years. One thousand dollars saved and earning 10 percent would grow to $45,000. Get the picture?

Wow! You don't have to be the next Warren Buffet to be a millionaire if you start early in life, invest in tax-advantaged accounts, and earn the average historical returns of the stock market.

The following is an example of how a college student (or any 20-something) with earnings could get an "extra" million-plus in retirement income.

Many people purchase a different car every three or four years. Usually this involves trading in a car and paying some additional amount for a newer, better car.

Imagine what could happen if you were to reduce the cost of your car trades by $5,000, purchasing a good but less expensive car. This would likely involve scaling back your hoped-for purchase and buying an older, less popular, or smaller car. Perhaps it means buying a $20,000 two-year-old used car instead of a new $25,000 current model, as you had hoped.

Now, let's say a typical college graduate will purchase cars at age 23, 27, 31, 35, and 39.... five purchases before 40 years of age. Further consider what could happen if he reduces his auto purchase costs and invested this $5,000 savings in a tax-sheltered investment that ends up compounding at 10 percent for 40 years for each of the investments.

The table below illustrates how the money would grow in this scenario.

Age	Money Saved ($)	10% for 40 Years	Future Sum ($) at Age
23	5,000	45×	225,000 at 63
27	5,000	45×	225,000 at 67
31	5,000	45×	225,000 at 71
35	5,000	45×	225,000 at 75
39	5,000	45×	225,000 at 79

This is a theoretical example of how individuals could modestly reduce their standard of living in return for substantial gains. In this case, $25,000 of savings before age 40 potentially turned into $1,125,000 in extra investment capital.

There is no guarantee this could actually occur because there are many variables: the ability to save, the ability to remain invested for many years, the ability to select investments and avoid current income taxation. However, though not a sure thing, this scenario is a possibility, and I know people who have lived this thrifty lifestyle and are multimillionaires as a result.

CHAPTER 9

Tracking Your Progress

What gets measured gets managed.

Tracking your progress is extremely helpful in realizing your goals. The everyday people I know who accumulated wealth on their own all had some very simple system for keeping track of their financial accounts.

Just keeping a record, say every six months, will help you stay focused on building your financial future. It is also a rewarding and encouraging feeling to be able to look back and realize how much you have achieved by monitoring your long-term results.

This chapter is a mini course in accounting, and it will help you track the growth of your financial world. The tool that accountants use to organize financial accounts is called one of several names: a financial statement or balance sheet or a net worth statement. No matter what name is used, here are the common elements:

Assets (things you own)
Liabilities (amounts you owe)
Net Worth (your true measure of wealth)

Here is a very simple example of what a net worth statement might look like:

Assets

Checking Account at Bank	$2,000
Savings Reserve Account	$5,000
Roth IRA Investment	$10,000
Stock in Company	$3,000
Car	$15,000
House	$150,000
Total Assets	**$185,000**

Liabilities

Car Loan	$8,000
Credit Card Balance	$2,000
Home Mortgage	$110,000
Total Liabilities	**$120,000**
Net Worth	**$65,000**

The formula is simple: Assets minus Liabilities equals Net Worth. Put simply, the value of what you own (your stuff) minus the value of what you owe (your loans) is your financial net worth.

As a reference point, get started right now by doing your own net worth statement as of today. Track this "net worth" number on a semiannual basis—January 1 and July 1 are easy dates to remember.

Assets

Checking Account   _____
Savings Accounts   _____
Insurance Cash Values   _____
Investment Accounts   _____
Retirement Accounts   _____
Automobiles   _____
Personal Items of Value   _____
Home   _____
Other Real Estate   _____
Other _____   _____
Other _____   _____
Other _____   _____

Total Assets   _____

Liabilities   _____

Credit Card Balances   _____
Car Loans   _____
Mortgage   _____
Loans to Others   _____
Other Amounts Owed   _____

Total Liabilities   _____

Net Worth   _____

Semiannual Net Worth Record

Date   Net Worth

Today $ _____
January 1, 20 ____ $ _____
July 1, 20 ____ $ _____
January 1, 20 ____ $ _____
July 1, 20 ____ $ _____
January 1, 20 ____ $ _____
July 1, 20 ____ $ _____

Hiring a Financial Planner to Help You Get Started

If you are having trouble making some financial decisions that are keeping you from getting started, you might want to pay someone to help you decide how much you should save, where you should start investing, what debts you should pay off, what investments you should be using, etc. This should be someone who will give you their recommendations in writing.

You might be best served by hiring a financial planner who charges you for advice on an hourly basis. An experienced adviser will probably charge you in the range of $100–300 per hour but will be able to help you make good choices and get you started on your way, right away.

If you do not know a fee-based financial planner, you could search the resources of these financial planning organizations and locate advisers in your area.

Certified Financial Planner Board of Standards
www.cfp.net

Financial Planning Association
www.fpanet.org

National Association of Personal Financial Advisors
www.napfa.org

CHAPTER 10

Five Financial Foundations for Life

Save some, spend some. Enjoy life while planning for your financial future.

When I started teaching college students about personal finance and developed the FFF for their use, I realized that helping them to just get started was the most important goal because most Americans do little to build their financial situation before age 30.

As we grow financially and earn more money, we become better equipped to use our "savings muscles," and the Five Financial Foundations goals can be bumped up.

If you're already saving and have your finances under control, you can step up your accumulation efforts and focus on greater financial progress.

To serve as a guide, I created the Stages of Life FFF chart below with suggested higher levels of savings, cash reserves, and financial goals to challenge Americans that are financially fit.

As you progress financially, consider developing a bigger, customized financial plan for you and your family. Put this plan into writing and review it often. A CERTIFIED FINANCIAL PLANNER™ Practitioner can help you to create this document.

Good luck as you improve your financial situation and make a better life for yourself and the people you love.

As stated in the introduction, this book is not intended to provide "one-size-fits-all" financial planning, but it's a good starting point for millions everywhere who are at the beginning of their financial life or have been delayed in getting started building their futures.

1	**Always Save** Reduce your lifestyle to allow "margin" for saving and investment	10% (min) of earnings Increase 1% annually
2	**Reserve Saving Cash** For emergencies, special purchases—avoid borrowing	10% of annual pay (min.) Begin car and home down payment fund
3	**Long-Term Investments** Employer benefits, tax-favored equity investments. Money to be invested for 8 yrs. or longer	Fund 401(k) to match; Roth contribution; purchase life insurance on favorable terms
4	**Rightsized Home** If you buy, 2–2 ½ annual income	Rent and save for 20% down payment (min.); use 30-yr. fixed rate mortgage if purchase home
5	**No Consumer Debt** No BAD: high-interest debt, nondeductible, purchase loses value	Elimininate all "bad" debt by age 30—or don't incur any

15% at 30 yrs. 20% at 35 yrs.	25–50% of earnings

Saving includes reserve savings cash, 401(k), 529 Plans, insurance overfunding, etc. ———

Use budgeting to understand spending ———

6-month living expenses; special-purchase savings accounts	1 year living expense plus cash for all major purchases and expenses for next 12 months

Use proper insurance of home, cars, property + earning (to protect cash reserve) ———

Fully fund company retirement plans; expand personal savings	Use substantial savings inflows to build personal retirement portfolio

10% compound for 40 yrs. multiplies 45× ——— Retirement savings target 25–30× annual living expenses

"Full-family" home purchase	Rightsize up or down; no debt by age 60 or retirement

Own home based on your *needs*, not your ego ———

Manageable "good" debt OK; pay cash for cars, clothes, special purchases; always pay off credit card balances	Pay cash for all purchases from portfolio or cash reserves

Debt is compound interest working *against* you ———